"Ghosts were created when the first man woke in the night."

-J.M. Barrie

A Teen's Guide to Ghost Hunting

Amanda R. Woomer

ISBN 979-8-362-77671-8

Printed in USA by Spook-Eats Publishing

For the future generation of ghost hunters... I look forward to working with you someday.

Other Titles by Amanda R. Woomer

The Feminine Macabre:
A Woman's Journal of All Things Strange & Unusual
The Feminine Macabre Volume II
The Feminine Macabre Volume III
The Feminine Macabre Volume IV

THE SPIRIT GUIDE SERIES:
America's Haunted Breweries, Distilleries, and Wineries
Harlots & Hauntings

A Very Frightful Victorian Christmas

A Haunted Atlas of Western New York

The Ghosts of the Ghostlight Theatre

Creepy Books for Creepy Kids:
The Cryptid ABC Book
Krampus's Great Big Book of Yuletide Monsters

A Teen's Guide to Ghost Hunting

Amanda R. Woomer

CONTENTS

Introduction

One: What is a Ghost? 1

Two: The History of Ghost Hunting 11

Three: Paranormal Activity 19

Four: Equipment 25

Five: Types of Locations 41

Six: Prepping for Your Hunt 53

Seven: Investigation Tips 59

Eight: Reviewing Evidence 89

Nine: The Paranormal Community 99

Ten: Recommended Reading 105

INTRODUCTION

So you want to begin your ghost hunting journey but are unsure where to start. I understand.

I had my first "paranormal experience" when I was seven years old. It scared me… but then it captured my imagination, and I couldn't stop thinking about it. I tried reading books on ghosts, aliens, cryptids, and unexplained phenomena, but the books were all written for adults, and I struggled to understand anything the authors were trying to say. When I was fourteen, paranormal reality TV took the world by storm, and I was finally able to grasp what had happened to me and what I was desperately trying to understand. But it doesn't take much time watching these types of shows to realize that they're purely for entertainment and you cannot learn much from them.

So how can we learn to investigate the paranormal safely? This book in your hands is here to help.

Young people and the paranormal go hand-in-hand, and they always have. Many researchers and investigators believe that infants and toddlers can see spirits—sometimes they manifest as "imaginary friends"—but eventually grow out of it. Many families tell stories of children and grandchildren talking about late family members that they've never met… yet still seem to know. Even poltergeist activity is said to sometimes revolve around pre-teens and teenagers as their bodies are going through puberty.

You have a place in the paranormal. You always have. And if you follow your passions and interests, you always will.

I can't say that this book will have all the answers for you—I've been doing this for nearly twenty years now (that's horrifying to admit), and I'm still learning new things—but I hope that it can be the first step in your paranormal journey.

The paranormal belongs to everyone—not just the famous people we see on TV and certainly not just grown-ups. I've gathered tips, tricks, and advice from members of the paranormal community that will have your back as you enter the incredible world of ghost hunting.

We can't wait to see what you do out there! Be safe. Be respectful. And have fun!

Amanda

AN IMPORTANT NOTE

The author of this book does not support or endorse trespassing to haunted locations. Before visiting any haunted site, you must obtain the proper permits/permission and respect private property and business hours.

Happy haunting!

A Teen's Guide to Ghost Hunting

Amanda R. Woomer

Chapter One
What is a Ghost?

Apparition. Spirit. Entity. Ghoul. Specter. Phantom.

There are many names associated with the idea of ghosts, and yet we're still not entirely sure what a ghost actually is. Ghosts can manifest in different ways and affect all of our senses:

> **FUN FACT:** The first depiction we have of a ghost is from an Ancient Babylonian tablet from 1500BCE.

You can see a ghost—sometimes they appear transparent, and others are as solid as you or me. There are instances of full-body apparitions as well as spirits appearing only partially, such as a pair of legs, a torso, or a headless ghost.

More often than not, you can hear a ghost. Many ghostly encounters include phantom footsteps, banging, music, crying, or someone even calling out your name.

You might feel a ghost in the form of cold spots in the environment, tingles, shivers, or even unseen hands tugging on your clothes or playing with your hair.

Sometimes, you might even smell a ghost, such as cigar smoke or their favorite perfume.

But that still doesn't answer the age-old question: what is a ghost?

The Spirit of the Dead

The most widely accepted belief is that a ghost is the presence of the dead.

Ghosts appear in different cultures worldwide and date back to ancient times. The idea of a supernatural world invisible to humans became popular during the Victorian Era (1820-1914) with the rise of mediums in the Spiritualist Movement and the publication of Charles Dickens's *A Christmas Carol*. The Victorians were obsessed

A Christmas Carol, *Marley's Ghost, John Leech, 1843*

with death and mourning for their loved ones. With mothers and babies that died in childbirth, diseases that killed children before we had vaccines, the American Civil War, the Spanish Flu pandemic, and World War I, death was an accepted part of life, and the belief that your loved ones were never far away acted as a comfort for grieving families.

Legends and lore surrounding ghosts claim that a spirit might come back for several reasons:

1. They don't realize that they're dead or may be traumatized by their death and cannot "move on."
2. They wish to be near their loved ones.
3. They're searching for closure or have unfinished business.
4. They seek revenge against someone who wronged them in life.

Thought-Forms

Thought-forms (sometimes also known as "tulpa") are considered artificial ghosts found in haunted locations. It's believed that they are created from concentrated human emotions in a specific place. An excellent example of this is Gettysburg, Pennsylvania.

Gettysburg National Battlefield
Photo courtesy of DJ Maschek

Imagine the young men charging across the battlefield, running towards cannons and muskets firing at them. Energy was coursing through their bodies in the form of emotions—courage, fear, adrenaline—and the moment a musket or cannonball hit them, that energy was released. Since we know that energy can't be created or destroyed, energy from the Battle of Gettysburg has remained long after the bodies have been carried away, making Gettysburg an extremely somber and heavy place to visit.

Some paranormal investigators, such as Richard Estep, believe that the haunting of the Villisca Axe Murder House is also a thought-form—people have been visiting this location in Villisca, Iowa, for years, trying to solve a 100-year-old murder mystery. When they arrive at the house, they bring their thoughts, theories, and passionate beliefs with them, and some of those emotions may stay behind.

Time-Slips

This is a supposed paranormal occurrence where you can see the same place you're standing but at a different point in time.

One of the most famous time-slips is documented in the book *An Adventure*, where two young women share their experience being transported from 1901 to 1792 while at the Palace of Versailles.

A recent example of a time-slip occurred on Bold Street in Liverpool, England—the most famous event happened in 1996. However, they still occur from time to time. In fact, there's a Reddit forum dedicated to Bold Street's time-slips.

FUN FACT: "Poltergeist" is German for "noisy ghost," and was first introduced to the English language by Catherine Crowe in 1847.

Humans like to see time in a linear way—it makes it easier for us to understand if we tell ourselves that yesterday is backward on the timeline and tomorrow is forward. But if you're a *Doctor Who* fan, you know time is wibbly-wobbly and more like a scribble than a straight line. Could a ghostly bride walking down the stairs of a "haunted" hotel be a point where two lines in time cross? She seems out of place to you… and you might seem out of place to her. Is it possible that we appear as ghosts on another timeline?

Time-slips are also sometimes used to explain the sensation of déjà vu.

An Imprint

You may have heard the expression "residual haunting." It's said to be the opposite of an "intelligent haunting," where the spirit can interact with the environment and people around it. Residual hauntings are an imprint or a recording absorbed by a building or space. This usually happens after a traumatic event, such as a battle, a murder, or an accident. When the situation is right, the recording begins to play, creating a haunting.

Sometimes, people report watching a ghost walk through walls and disappear, oblivious to its surroundings.

This is a great example of a residual haunting and likely shows the imprint is following an old path along a hallway that might no longer exist due to remodeling in a house.

A term you might hear associated with imprints and residual hauntings is the "Stone Tape Theory," which suggests that a building's materials, such as wood and stone, can also absorb the energy of people and events and play them back over time.

Demons?

If you've watched paranormal TV recently, you've heard the word "demon" thrown around a few (hundred) times. But where does this terrifying concept come from?

According to traditional Protestant beliefs, when a person dies, their soul goes to one of two places: Heaven if they were a good person and Hell if they were a bad person. This was (and still is) a black-and-white take on life after death, leaving no room for ghosts to wander among humans. Because of this, many believe that ghosts are actually entities sent by the Devil to trick you.

Like ghosts, demons are found in many cultures worldwide and aren't always considered evil. In fact, the word "demon" means "replete with wisdom" or "full of wisdom." "Demon" comes from the Greek word *daimon,* meaning a guiding spirit or deity, and does not have the negative meaning seen today.

In the 21st Century, the term "non-human entity" has grown in popularity and is helping the paranormal field venture beyond the Christian perspective. This label is used to describe any presence that is not human (aka a ghost), such as elementals, deities, thought-forms (positive or negative), and guardians (such as angels).

In Japanese folklore, household objects (such as this paper lantern) can become possessed by a spirit and become Tsukumogami. *Circa 1830.*

It's important to remember that just because you come into contact with something negative doesn't mean it's a demon. If you were kind in life, you'd be kind in death. And if you were a jerk in life, you'd likely be a jerk in death. You should always be wary of who or what you're potentially communicating with, but don't think that everything you encounter is a demon.

There are several other theories and ideas of what might create the paranormal phenomena we experience while investigating, such as aliens and even humanity's collective consciousness. It's impossible to know just what it is that creates paranormal activity, such as apparitions, strange sounds, phantom smells, psychic feelings, and electronic voice phenomenon (EVP). Perhaps one day, you'll be the one to figure it out.

Chapter Two
The History of Ghost Hunting

Ghost hunting is not a new concept. Since the mid-2000s, paranormal TV shows have grown in popularity, but the truth is that people have been trying to find ways to prove life after death exists for… well… forever.

With folklore and superstition surrounding the deaths and supposed afterlives of friends and families, it's safe to say that humans have been fascinated with the supernatural for millennia. Ghost stories seem to be part of human nature:

One of our earliest documented ghost stories comes from Pliny the Younger in the 1st Century and recounts a paranormal experience had by Athenodorus Canaanites (an ancient philosopher who lived from 74 BCE to 7CE). The story tells of his time renting a haunted house in Athens, where the ghost of a thin man covered in chains appeared to him. Athenodorus eventually followed the spirit to his courtyard, where he found a skeleton wrapped in chains buried there.

In Ancient Egypt, many people wrote letters to the dead, seeking advice or sharing their personal problems.

Before the spread of Christianity, ghosts were seen as a natural part of the world—though they could be mischievous and troublesome at times.

In 856, the first poltergeist was documented in a tiny farmhouse in Germany, tormenting the family that lived there.

Norse and European mythology told of the Wild Hunt, where ghosts, demons, and gods would ride through the night, and if a mortal saw them, it would bring war and death.

Stories quickly spread of Anne Boleyn's headless ghost wandering around the Tower of London after she was executed in 1536.

Shortly after George Washington died, visitors who spent the night in his former bedroom at Mount Vernon reported seeing the nation's first president's ghostly image.

The Victorians loved telling ghost stories at Christmas time—the most famous being Dickens's *A Christmas Carol.*

Women in White are said to sadly wander through cemeteries. Gray Ladies tend to haunt grand manors in the English countryside. Soldiers are seen and heard still fighting on battlefields. Phantom hitchhikers are seen along roads.

Ghosts are part of our lives in books and movies, the stories we tell around the campfire, and the legends that make up our unique cultures.

But when did we start hunting ghosts to see if we could find evidence of life after death?

The answer comes from Edinburgh, Scotland, in 1854 when a woman named Catherine Crowe conducted the very first paranormal investigation as we know it today. Catherine and her team (including a psychic medium) investigated an apartment building that couldn't seem to keep tenants. They attempted not just to make contact with the other side, but to try to understand what was happening, how it was happening, and why it was happening. Catherine was also the author of the first reference book on the paranormal, published one year before the Spiritualist Movement's start, bringing the paranormal into the limelight. *The Night-Side of Nature* (1847) attempted to collect first-hand accounts of phenomena such as ghosts, wraiths, and poltergeists.

The only known image of Catherine Crowe.

Another notable early paranormal investigator was Charles Fort, who studied strange phenomena at the turn of the 20th Century. He wrote on levitation, spontaneous human combustion, unidentified flying objects, teleportation (a term credited directly to Fort), and unidentified submerged objects in oceans. His research also included hauntings, ghosts, and poltergeists, but his work was so unique that it created a cult following, and now, the word "Fortean" (clearly derived from Fort's last name) is sometimes used to describe unexplainable events.

As mentioned in Chapter One, during the 19th Century, people were obsessed with death. This led to the Spiritualist Movement, which insisted that when someone died, they were not sent to purgatory, nor did they disappear into Heaven or Hell. Instead, ordinary people (both men *and* women) could communicate with the dead and bring messages to families. People no longer required pastors and priests to connect to the other side. The Spiritualist Movement led to an increase in séances, psychic mediums, and (sadly) con artists. To combat fake mediums that were taking advantage of grieving families, the Society for Psychical Research (SPR)

The author at the birthplace of Spiritualism just outside of Rochester, New York.

was founded in 1882. This was the first established attempt to document and understand paranormal activity in a scientific and non-religious way. The men and women of the SPR studied physical mediums, spirit photographers, hypnotists, slate writers, claims of telepathy, automatic writing, haunted houses, and other psychic powers. The society was (and still is) made up of individuals with backgrounds in psychology, mathematics, chemistry, poetry, philosophy, art, and physics. Even Harry Houdini and Sir Arthur Conan Doyle (the author of *Sherlock Holmes*) were interested in researching (and, in Houdini's case, debunking) paranormal phenomena.

Houdini and the ghost of Abraham Lincoln. *This double exposure photo demonstrated how a photographer could produce a fraudulent "spirit photo." LC-USZ62-26516*

Examples of spirit photography from (in)famous photographers John K. Hallowell (upper left), William Mumler (upper right), William Hope, (lower left), and Frederick A. Hudson (lower right).

As the 20th Century continued, advances in things like film and photography made investigating the paranormal easier and more accessible. Other notable 20th Century investigators were Harry Price, Hans Holzer, and the controversial Ed and Lorraine Warren (who you might recognize from *The Conjuring* horror movie franchise).

Ghost hunting entered the mainstream when paranormal reality TV shows began to appear in the early 2000s, and the rest (as they say) is history.

Today, investigators are known to incorporate hi-tech 21st Century gadgets with old-fashioned tools and methods such as talking boards. In Chapter Four, we'll talk about some of the equipment and techniques that continue to build on the history of ghost hunting.

Chapter Three
Paranormal Activity

As mentioned in Chapter One, there are many ways to experience a haunting through all of our senses.

Sight

Visually, you might witness paranormal activity in the form of shadow people (dark figures) and light anomalies (such as rods of light, bursts of light, or balls of light, also known as "orbs"). You might also experience physical objects moving around you by unseen hands. People commonly report doors opening and closing on their own, lights turning off and on, balls rolling (especially if a child spirit is said to haunt the location), objects flying off walls or shelves, and sometimes objects being thrown. Of course, the

> **TIP:** BEWARE OF ORBS! It's one thing to see a ball of light with your own eyes, and it's another thing to "catch" an orb in a photo. 99% of the time, orbs in photos can be explained by moisture in the air, pollen, dust, or bugs. Very rarely do they offer any sort of proof of a haunting… just a need to dust!

pinnacle of paranormal activity is seeing a full-body apparition, though this does not happen nearly as frequently as we'd like to admit (though it does happen from time to time).

A photo with dozens of orbs taken at Gettysburg College by the author. The fact that the photo was taken outside at night should tell you that the orbs are most likely not paranormal but moisture in the air reflected in the flash.

Sound

One of the most common ways to experience the paranormal is through sounds. There are two ways to experience noises while investigating the paranormal.

The first way is in real-time or while you are investigating. You might hear footsteps when no one else is around or knocks on walls or doors. Some investigators hear whispers, voices, and sometimes even laughter or screams. This is known as audible voice phenomenon (shortened to AVP). You might also hear a door slam or even unexplainable music.

The second way to experience sound while investigating is through audio recordings. Also known as electronic voice phenomenon (shortened to EVP), this occurs when a voice can only be heard on audio equipment and not with your own ears. Many times, while on a ghost hunt, investigators will conduct an EVP session where they record a conversation while they ask questions and wait to see if they get an answer… and sometimes they do. [We'll talk more about the equipment needed for an EVP session and how to conduct one successfully in Chapters Four and Seven.]

Touch

Some people report feeling a ghost. This could be as cold spots or the sensation of physical touch.

While investigating, you may experience something referred to as a "cold spot." While cold spots are not inherently paranormal (always check for open windows, doors, and drafts), if there is no logical explanation, a drop in temperature could be a spirit trying to manifest.

It is also possible to experience the sensation of someone touching you. This could be in the form of an unseen entity tugging on your clothes (particularly when a child ghost is present) or someone playing with your hair or possibly even tugging it. Another peculiar sensation ghost hunters might experience is described as tingles or even the feeling of walking through a spider web (when there isn't one around, of course). There are occasional reports of people being bitten, hit, or scratched, but this doesn't happen as frequently as paranormal media would have you believe.

SMELL

> **TIP:** Don't be discouraged if others can't smell what you smell. You might have a psychic gift called "clairalience," which means you can tap into psychic information through your sense of smell!

Believe it or not, you can also smell a ghost! Many reports from haunted locations include phantom smells such as pipe tobacco, flowers, cigars, rose and lavender perfume, smoke, and sometimes even rotten eggs and fish. It's important to make sure that the odor you smell has no possible source—that will reveal whether this is paranormal, if an animal has died, leading to a putrid smell, or if someone is smoking nearby. It is also recommended that you avoid wearing perfume or anything scented (such as shampoo or deodorant) when investigating, so it's not mistaken for a phantom scent. Unlike sight and sound, smell is a particularly difficult sense to measure and collect data on (along with touch), but you should still try to document when you smell something that seems out of place in your surroundings.

There's a popular expression among paranormal investigators which says that your body is your best tool. You don't have to be psychic to experience a ghost with your body—as long as you're open, calm, and paying attention, you might smell, feel, hear, or even see something otherworldly!

Chapter Four
Equipment

It's a common misconception (even among adults) that you need the newest and most expensive gadgets to have a successful ghost hunt. You might see SLS cameras, DR-60 digital recorders, thermal imaging cameras, and "portals" on TV. Many of these pieces of equipment can cost thousands of dollars. And while they might help in an investigation (the success of particular gadgets is debatable), you certainly don't need to spend a fortune on your ghost hunting kit. Here are some of my favorite pieces of equipment for under $100, as well as some things you might already have.

Your Smart Phone

You may not think of ghost hunts when you're playing on your phone, but it's the perfect starting point when you're new to investigating. In fact, it's a three-in-one tool.

It's a camera, and depending on your phone type, your camera might be better than some professional cameras out there. Many times, people unknowingly capture images of ghosts while snapping photos on their phones, so be ready!

It's a flashlight. Many times, when you're investigating, the lights will be out (this could be because the location doesn't have electricity or you choose to turn the lights off to make it extra spooky). It's always wise to have at least one flashlight with you. Before investing in a flashlight (I prefer red ones because they're easier on your eyes), your phone's flashlight will work just fine.

It's a digital recorder. iPhones have a voice memo app, and Androids have a sound recorder app. While it may not catch as wide a range of sound as more advanced recording equipment, it's perfect for short EVP sessions and can still catch the occasional voice or thump you might not be able to hear with your ears.

While phones can be handy on an investigation, there are two things to keep in mind:

1. **Always put your phone in airplane mode.** If you don't, any time your phone gets a message, notification, or turns on, it could potentially interfere with equipment, leading to a false reading.

2. **Avoid ghost hunting apps.** These apps, while entertaining, cannot be trusted if you're genuinely trying to investigate the paranormal. Certain apps have been known to be fake when claiming to find/track ghosts. Your phone often has geotracking turned on and knows if you're in a cemetery or a supposedly haunted location. Phones also like to listen to us when we talk and will learn how to answer any questions you might ask in a ghost hunting app.

Tarot

Tarot cards have experienced a revival over the last few years as a way to potentially communicate with spirits while on an investigation.

You can use court cards (the King, Queen, Knight, and Page) to learn more about the spirit and their personality.

You can use the pip cards (the numbered cards) to ask questions like:

"What message do you have for me?"

"What do you need?"

"What were you like in life?"

"What do I need to know about you or this place?"

Waite-Smith Tarot Deck from 1909.
Photo courtesy of Nosferattus

You might also want to take note of the types of cards that appear—multiple suits or numbers can mean something.

The Waite-Smith tarot deck is the most popular deck and costs less than $20. Many practitioners have multiple decks that they use for different reasons. Find the one that works best for you and practice reading the cards… they're a unique tool!

Cat Balls

Believe it or not, those light-up plastic balls you watch your cat bat around the house can double as ghost hunting equipment.

It's a simple concept: when the ball sits still, it's dark, and the minute it moves, it lights up. Investigators use these little toys to document potential paranormal phenomena, such as the ball rolling on its own or ghostly footsteps on a nearby surface.

These tools cost about $5 and can be just as valuable as the much more expensive tools that detect movement (which usually start at about $200).

Audio Recorders

Audio recorders are a staple for most ghost hunters on any investigation. As far as equipment goes, they're relatively affordable, with the cheaper ones running about $30. Some audio recorders come with a USB port that allows you to transfer your files to a computer where you can more easily review them. However, this is unnecessary, so if yours doesn't have that option, don't worry—if you think you caught an EVP, you can always record it onto your phone and then transfer it to your computer.

Some investigators prefer using old-fashioned tape recorders for their EVP sessions. According to John E.L. Tenney, this is because digital recorders work in the binary and sound waves on a digital recorder look more like a staircase than a perfect wave as recorded on cassette tapes. In theory, you can pick up more sounds and possibly more voices on a cassette than on a digital recorder. Portable cassette recorders cost about $20 online, and you can also find cassette tapes for about $5. If you're unsure how to work your cassette recorder, ask your parents—they'll be thrilled to see this blast from their past!

When I first started investigating in 2004, I still used my family's cassette recorder. My first digital recorder was an Olympus—not too expensive, but I caught some interesting things. Especially when you're just starting, you don't have to spend hundreds (or even thousands) of dollars on recorders.

When using an audio recorder on an investigation, it is essential to "tag" noises that you hear during your session that have a logical explanation. This could be a car driving by, someone sniffling, your stomach growling, or someone shifting in their chair. We'll talk more about the importance of tagging sounds in Chapter Seven.

Dowsing Rods

Dowsing rods (along with other tools such as Ouija boards and pendulums) are a controversial tool in the ghost hunter's bag of tricks. Some investigators love to use them, while others claim that the person holding the device unconsciously manipulates it (known as the ideomotor effect).

Using dowsing rods is simple: stand perfectly still while holding one rod in each hand, keeping them parallel to the floor. When you ask yes or no questions, the rods will cross and push away as the spirit supposedly answers your questions.

Dowsing rods are simple tools used for centuries (originally used to find water). You can usually purchase a set for about $15 or a combo pack with rods and a pendulum for $20.

When using the rods, it's important to remember there is always a chance that you are manipulating them, whether you mean to or not.

K2 Meters

If you've ever attended a public ghost hunt or watched paranormal TV shows, you've likely seen a K2 meter in action.

TIP: Side effects of high EMF exposure include nausea, headaches, and even hallucinations... which can be mistaken for a haunting.

About the size of a TV remote, K2 meters detect electromagnetic fields (usually shortened to EMF) and show you the levels based on green, yellow, orange, and red lights. Other types of tools pick up on electromagnetic fields, such as EMF meters and REM-Pods.

Initially used by electricians to make sure wires were dead before working on them, EMF meters are also used by people who want to keep an eye on the levels of electromagnetic radiation around their homes. Today, EMF meters have become a popular tool among ghost hunters.

It's believed that ghosts give off energy, so if the lights on a K2 meter or a REM-Pod change without any logical explanation, it could be a sign of a presence nearby.

FUN FACT: Our bodies also have electromagnetic fields (even if they are very weak). This has led some researchers to believe that ghosts do as well.

Before using a K2 meter or any other EMF meter, you'll want to "sweep" the room—make your way around the room to see what the base reading is and make a note of any areas with bad wiring or electronic devices which will also give off a high reading. Once you do this, you'll better understand what readings are normal and what might be paranormal.

K2 meters cost about $25, while other EMF meters can run $50-100+.

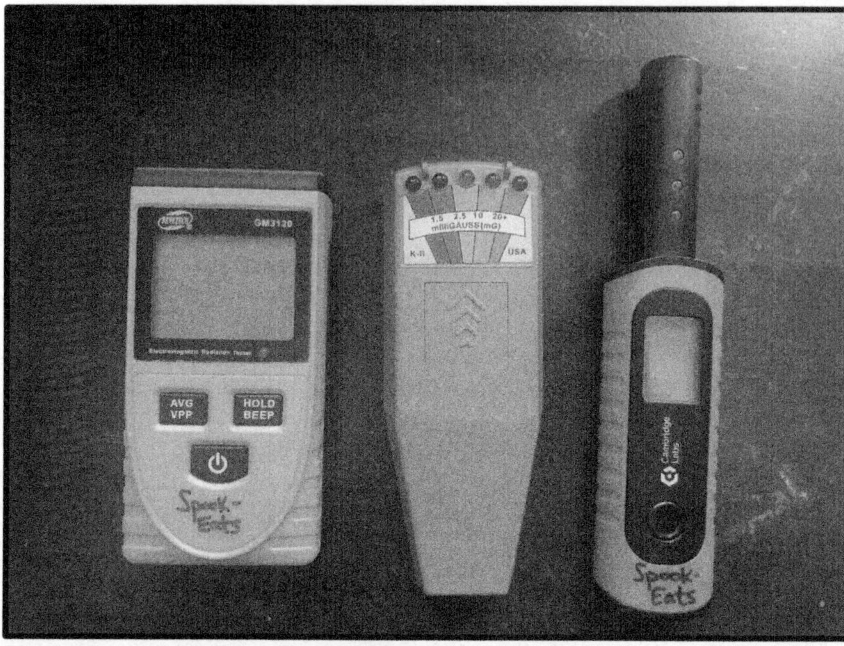

Three types of EMF meters with the K2 meter in the center.

Spirit Box (SB-7)

The SB-7 (also known as the spirit box) has become extremely popular among ghost hunting groups over the last few years. There are other versions of this equipment, such as the "Shack Hack" radio and the SBox spirit box. I have gotten some interesting results from the SB-7 and the SB-7T.

Spirit boxes sweep through AM and FM radio stations at a fraction of a second, creating a form of white noise. Theories claim that if you hear a voice coming through, it's not from the radio but rather a spirit voice coming through over multiple radio stations. There have been instances of words and even complete sentences that have come through this way. It is similar to an EVP session but in real-time.

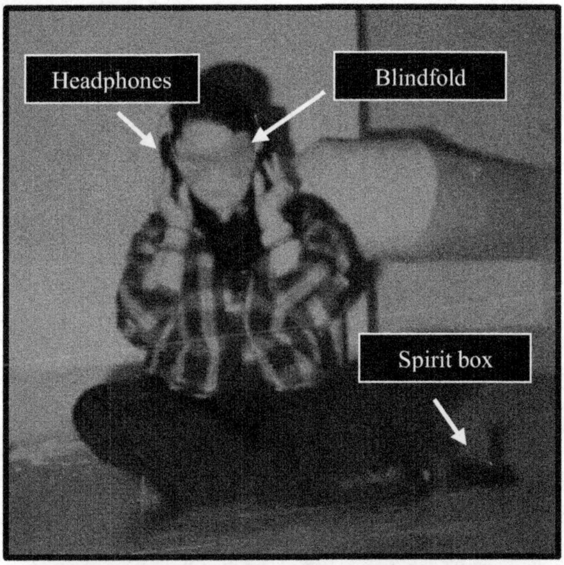

The author during an Estes Method session at Madison Seminary in 2021. Note the headphones, blindfold, and spirit box to her left-hand side.

Spirit boxes are sometimes used for Estes Method sessions. This is when one investigator "goes under" and puts on a blindfold and a pair of headphones attached to the spirit box. It is the listener's job to try to hear any voices or words that might come through and say them out loud for everyone else to hear. The rest of the team (unable to listen to the spirit box) asks a series of questions and waits to see if the listener hears a response. This method guarantees that the person listening to the response does not know the question, making potential intelligent responses more impressive (and avoiding similar issues as seen with dowsing rods and Ouija boards).

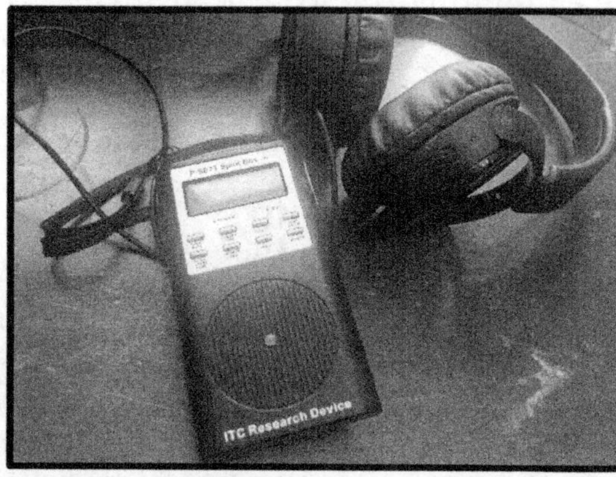

The SB-7T

Spirit boxes can cost different prices, with the SB-7 running about $89 and the SBox about $99.

The Portal

This piece of equipment breaks my "keep it under $100" rule, but I want to show you how you can make your own for relatively cheap, and it's an interesting and fun piece of equipment to bring on a ghost hunt. These hi-tech gadgets can sometimes cost up to $800, but this tutorial will keep it around $200 (even less if you already own a spirit box!).

Portals (or as I like to call them, "spirit radios") incorporate a spirit box such as the SB-7/SB-7T and use everyday pieces of technology to filter out the white noise so only "voices" come through. This makes it easier to listen to and more enjoyable if you're prone to headaches caused by loud noises.

What you will need:

-one SB-7 ($89)

-two ¼-inch male to 1/8-inch male aux cables (about $10 each)

-a guitar noise gate pedal ($35)

-a ¼-inch patch cable ($10)

-a reverb pedal ($40)

-a speaker (ranges from $30 up to $100. Remember the higher the watts, the louder it will be)

-9-volt battery power supply for pedals (you can use a daisy chain if you want to cut costs and don't mind plugging into an outlet).

What to do:

1. Plug the 1/8-inch side of the aux cable into the SB-7.
2. Plug the ¼-inch side of the aux cable into the noise gate pedal input.
3. Plug the patch cable into the noise gate output.
4. Plug the other end of the patch cable into the reverb pedal input.
5. Plug the ¼-inch side of the second aux cable into the reverb output.
6. Plug the 1/8-inch side of the second aux cable into the speaker.
7. Power on the SB-7, noise gate, reverb pedal, and speaker, and get chatting!

I put my portal inside an antique radio to make it look more familiar to the spirits I might be talking to. Check out the finished product in the next image.

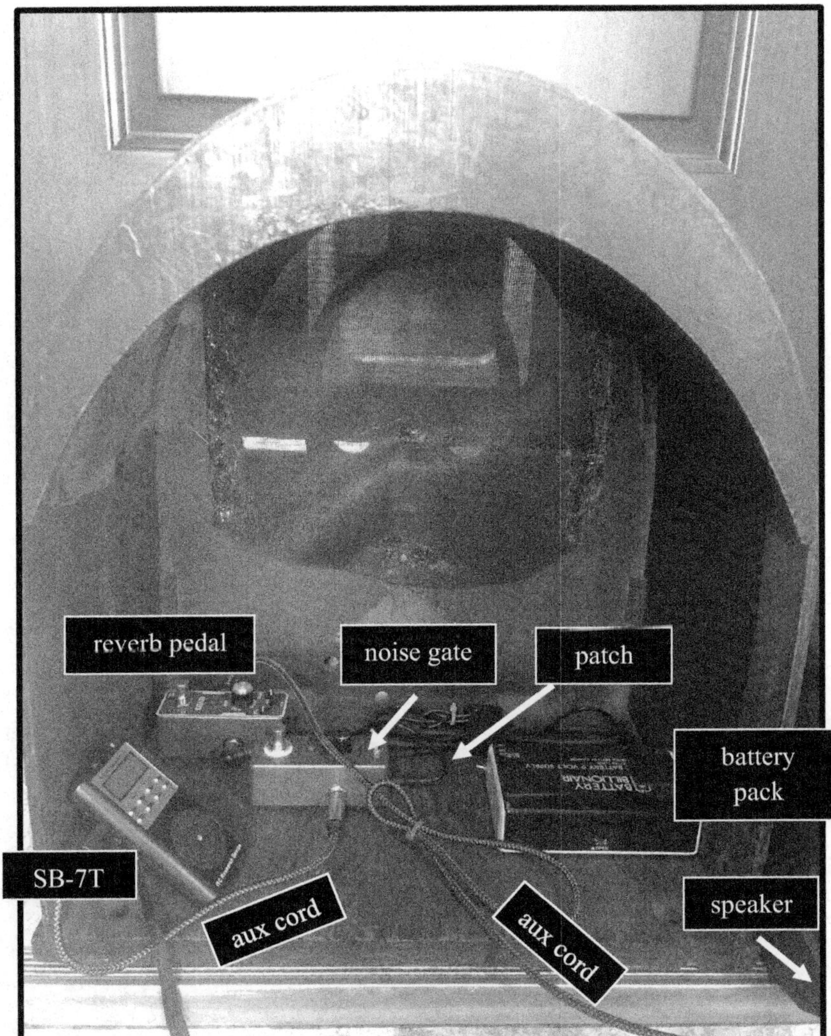
reverb pedal
noise gate
patch
battery pack
SB-7T
aux cord
aux cord
speaker

Chapter Five
Types of Locations

There are a variety of locations you can investigate, however, the most important thing to remember is to never trespass. Urbexing (urban exploring) is popular now, but it can be extremely dangerous and even lead to financial problems that your parents won't appreciate. It's always safest to get permission to visit private locations. There are also several types of haunted places open to the public.

Asylums

These are perhaps some of the most (in)famous haunted locations in the country, and many of them are open for investigations.

Asylums became particularly popular during the Victorian Era when it was believed that people deemed "mad" should be separated from society where they could then be helped. It was a nice theory, but the living conditions were often horrible, the staff was overwhelmed and sometimes cruel, and patients rarely ever got the help they needed. Today, we know many of these "insane" patients had very normal medical conditions, such as epilepsy or depression, or some were simply grieving the loss of a loved one.

The Buffalo State Asylum was built in 1870.

Some asylums open for public events and private investigations are the Trans Allegheny Lunatic Asylum in Weston, West Virginia, Pennhurst Asylum in Spring City,

Pennsylvania, and Rolling Hills Asylum in East Bethany, New York. The upper floor of Madison Seminary in Madison, Ohio, is also referred to as The Asylum.

Madison Seminary in Madison, OH.

SANATORIUM/SANITARIUM

Wildwood Sanitarium in Salamanca, NY.

Two different spellings, but they mean the same thing—it's just an old-fashioned name for a hospital designed to help a specific type of disease. Most of the time, sanatoriums were used to house patients with tuberculosis (which, before antibiotics, was an extremely contagious disease). Other times, they helped people with addictions. Like asylums, they grew in popularity during the Victorian Age, but by the mid-20th Century, we had discovered an antibiotic for tuberculosis, and sanatoriums were no longer necessary.

Many of these historic buildings were either transformed into apartments, senior citizen centers, or abandoned. Luckily, a few have been preserved—they share their history and ghost stories with anyone interested to know more.

Wildwood Sanitarium in Salamanca, New York, Waverly Hills Sanatorium in Louisville, Kentucky, and Cresson Sanatorium in Lilly, Pennsylvania, are all open for public and private events for you to visit and explore.

THEATRES

Thanks to stories like *The Phantom of the Opera*, theatres have become one of the most haunted places in the world. And why not? Hundreds (sometimes even thousands) of people come and go as audience members. Actors pretend to be different people, dressing up in period costumes, possibly stirring up memories for the spirits present. Actors produce

emotions such as fear and sadness while on stage, and audience members laugh, cry, and occasionally scream… that energy must go somewhere. Add lights, computers, speakers, extension cords, cables, and wires (all things paranormal investigators believe can feed ghosts), and you have the perfect environment for a haunting.

Most theatres embrace their ghost stories (theatre people tend to be very superstitious), so a theatre is a great place to investigate! Many theatres offer ghost tours and ghost hunts, such as The Fowler Theatre in Fowler, Indiana, The Canton Palace Theatre in Canton, Ohio, and (my personal favorite) The Ghostlight Theatre in North Tonawanda, New York.

FUN FACT: Every theatre has a "ghostlight" which is a light that always stays on in order to keep the ghosts from causing mischief.

Poor Houses

You'll start to notice a theme about poorly planned institutes during the Victorian Era, and poor houses were another example of that. Popular in England, Wales, and Ireland, poor houses (sometimes known as almshouses) were also used in the United States and Canada to house people who could not support themselves. Run mainly by the counties, most people who lived and worked in poor houses and on poor farms were elderly or disabled, and their needs were never met. Many of these facilities were infested with mice and vermin, were overcrowded, filthy, and provided little ventilation, making them hazardous places to live.

After the Social Security Act in 1935, most poor houses were closed, and by 1950, they were completely gone.

Today, most poor houses are abandoned and are unsafe to visit alone. However, Rolling Hills Asylum was originally a poor house, and the Greene County Poor Farm in Waynesburg, Pennsylvania, Ashmore Estates in Ashmore, Illinois, and Hill View Manor in New Castle, Pennsylvania, are safe to visit with various tour groups such as Ghosts N'at Paranormal Adventures, American Hauntings, and Ghost Hunts USA.

Hotels

Not all haunted locations have to be spooky. Hotels are considered "liminal" or places where no one stays for too long (hallways, staircases, and roads are also liminal), and liminal spaces tend to have ghost stories attached.

If you think of the number of people who have come and gone through hotels over the centuries, you can see why some might be haunted.

Some of the most famous haunted hotels are the Hawthorne Hotel in Salem, Massachusetts, the Stanly Hotel in Estes Park, Colorado (which inspired Stephen King to write *The Shining*), the Crescent Hotel in Eureka Springs, Arkansas, and the Farnsworth House in Gettysburg, Pennsylvania. These locations are great to visit if you're spending the night—you'll get a sense of what the building feels like while also enjoying things like heat, electricity, and plumbing, which aren't always available at other locations!

Cemeteries

There's an old legend that says the last person to be buried in a cemetery must stand guard and watch over the dead until the next person is buried and they can finally rest. If this is true, then every cemetery is haunted.

However, if you plan to visit a cemetery, the most important thing you can do is be respectful. Often, these are active cemeteries where families come to bury their dead while others are grieving. And even if it is a historic cemetery and no longer active, it should still be treated as sacred because it is.

Charter Street Cemetery (aka the Old Burying Point) in Salem, Massachusetts.

It *is* possible to investigate a cemetery or a specific grave, but you must be wise. If there are other people around, rethink your plan. It's also recommended that you research the cemetery's rules and regulations when investigating the paranormal—some cemeteries embrace their haunted history while others oppose it.

> **FUN FACT:** What's the difference between a cemetery and a graveyard? A graveyard is usually attached to a church while a cemetery stands on its own.

Some of the more famous haunted and just plain spooky cemeteries are St. Louis Cemetery #1 in New Orleans, Louisiana, Hollywood Forever Cemetery in Los Angeles, California, Union Cemetery in Easton, Connecticut, Bonaventure Cemetery in Savannah, Georgia, and Greyfriars Kirkyard in Edinburgh, Scotland.

My advice would be to visit a cemetery to do historical research into a haunting or to enjoy your surroundings. There are plenty of other places to pull out your K2 meter or audio recorder… a cemetery might not be the best place.

Greyfriars Kirkyard... home to the Mackenzie Poltergeist and one of the few cemeteries open 24 hours.

There are other types of places that can be haunted, such as:

Restaurants

Battlefields

Houses

Reformatories/Prisons

Hospitals

Orphanages

Roads

Bridges

Parks

Churches

Forts

Ships

Hiking paths

Entire towns

TIP: Many roads, such as Pigman Road in New York and Boy Scout Lane in Wisconsin, have ghost stories attached to them. Please be extremely careful anytime you're near a road. There have been instances where ghost hunters have died after being hit by cars during nighttime investigations.

Chapter Six
Prepping for Your Hunt

Prepping for a ghost hunt can seem daunting (it gets easier over time… I promise)—not only do you physically have to prepare your gear, but you have to mentally prepare yourself for possibly coming into contact with the paranormal. Here are some things to remember while prepping for your ghost hunt.

Find the Right Event for You

Not all paranormal experiences are created equal.

When you're just starting out investigating the paranormal, you don't want to pay hundreds of dollars for a private investigation—you want to know how a ghost hunt should be run before you set out on your own. You should attend several public ghost hunts before committing to a private one.

Paranormal tourism is popular right now, with groups running public events for newbie investigators throughout the year (but especially around Halloween). Be sure to read reviews on these groups because some events are run better than others. Also, remember that some of these events are only available for adults. Others might allow teens to join in, but only if a parent or guardian is with them, so you might have to bring mom or dad with you.

Research

This is debatable. Some people like to research the location they're going to visit, while others like to go in "blind."

Both approaches have positives and negatives—if you research names or dates, that could unintentionally lead you to look for specific answers, but if you don't know any details, you might miss important information while investigating.

Your research can begin with a simple Google search, but I recommend going beyond that. Your local library is your friend, so be sure to check it out—there are books, newspaper articles, census records, and more available through your library, and a librarian will be more than happy to help you with your research.

Personally, I like to research the history of a location beforehand because (to me) it provides a more well-rounded experience. I can connect with potential spirits on a more personal level, which might lead to better results in the investigation. Additionally, there are times when historical records might confirm a ghost story or completely debunk it.

It might be a fun experiment to go to one location "blind" and another after thoroughly researching it and seeing what works best for you.

Charge Your Batteries

It might seem obvious, but this step sometimes gets overlooked, even by experienced ghost hunters.

Some equipment must be plugged in to charge (cameras, some EMF meters, and some digital recorders), while most (K2 meters, SB-7s, some audio recorders, and some REM-Pods) require batteries.

Instead of using single-use batteries that you throw away after they've drained, consider buying rechargeable batteries and a charging station. Eventually, you'll save money, and you can bring the charger with you if you need it… and if one theory is correct, you'll most likely need it.

It's believed that ghosts will drain batteries to either manifest or cause activity, so make sure you bring plenty of batteries with you.

Protection

Protection can come in many forms within the paranormal.

> **TIP:** "Smudging" with white sage is a closed practice, so unless you've been properly instructed by an Indigenous elder, use other herbs like dill, lavender, nettle, parsley, or oregano.

Some people are nervous about coming into contact with the "other side," so they choose to protect themselves spiritually. If you are religious, you might wear or carry something like a cross or a Hamsa/evil eye. Some people carry crystals that supposedly have protective qualities (amethyst, clear quartz, obsidian, black tourmaline, and jade, to name just a few). You might say a prayer or visualize a bright white light surrounding you. Some people like to (safely) burn incense or palo santo wood (my personal preference). Others might draw a sigil and put it in their pocket to ward off negativity.

When thinking of ways to protect yourself on an investigation, you'll also want to protect yourself physically. Always wear closed-toed shoes whether you're investigating inside or outside. Many times, these locations are not maintained, and you could step on a nail, screw, or broken glass, trip on uneven floors, or stumble down dark staircases. Also, consider that many locations do not have heat, so you'll want to dress warmly in the colder months—layers are always a good idea.

Lastly, make sure you protect yourself against questionable situations and people. It's an unfortunate truth that there are some bad people in the paranormal community (like all communities) that might try to hurt, abuse, or take advantage of you. Make sure you attend these events with people you trust, and never go off on your own or with anyone you're not comfortable with. These instances are extremely rare (since 2004, I've never had an issue). However, they do happen on occasion, so be safe and smart.

The author's personal protection box she carries in a fanny pack on every investigation. It is filled with dill and other herbs, a palo santo stick, and a piece of quartz. Also shown is her Hamsa/evil eye bracelet she wears.

Chapter Seven
Investigation Tips

There is nothing quite like the thrill of a ghost hunt—your heart will be pounding loud enough to hear it in your ears, you'll likely get scared at least a few times, and (if you're lucky) you might even come into contact with a spirit.

Luckily, if you attend public events run by a company, many times, they will take care of things for you—providing equipment, preparing the equipment, and knowing the layout of the location. However, if you've advanced to a private hunt, make sure you've prepared your equipment, gotten familiar with the area before turning off the lights, and set up your "base camp" where you can keep your gadgets when you're not using them, as well as snacks, drinks, toiletries, and any medication you might need. Often, a private hunt will include a walkthrough tour with someone familiar with the grounds so you won't get lost.

The more investigations you go on, the more comfortable and confident you'll become. But for those just starting, here are some tips to keep in mind for a successful and rewarding ghost hunt.

The Golden Rule

The most important thing you can do while trying to interact with a ghost is to treat them like a person… because, at one point in time, they were (that is, if we believe the theory that they're the presence of the deceased as discussed in Chapter One).

You'd likely run and hide if someone came into your home and started shouting and swearing. This is why provocation is always a bad idea regarding the paranormal. It can either cause spirits to avoid you or lash out at you—neither of which you want to happen.

Instead, think of them as a person—someone's child, parent, or lover—and treat them with the respect that you'd like to experience yourself. Many times, when we slow down and try to get to know the spirits supposedly haunting a place, the results can be incredible.

Never Go Alone

This goes back to our section on protection and should be a general rule in all aspects of life—not just the paranormal! When you're on a ghost hunt, always make sure you have at least one person with you. This is for several reasons:

- **Safety.** You'll likely be unfamiliar with the location's layout, and there is always a possibility that you might hurt yourself—you could trip down a dark flight of stairs or twist your ankle—or get lost.
- **Evidence.** If you encounter an entity or other paranormal phenomena, you'll have someone to help support your claims.
- **It's more fun!** Let's be honest: experiences (especially of the supernatural variety) are always more fun when shared.

Put Your Phone in Airplane Mode

I mentioned this in Chapter Three, but it's so important (and simple!) I'll remind you:

Put your phone in airplane mode.

Anytime you get a text or notification or your phone wakes up, it can affect equipment and give you a false reading. This could be particularly disappointing when you think you're communicating with a spirit, but you're really just getting updates on your favorite sports team.

Taking Photos

Even though orbs caught in photos aren't paranormal, that doesn't mean you can't capture interesting anomalies in your photos. And you don't have to spend a fortune to get the perfect camera either. A full spectrum camera (that captures all light on the spectrum, not just infrared or visible light) can cost around $200. However, people have been able to catch some exciting things on Polaroid cameras and smartphones.

When taking photos on a ghost hunt, it's always wise to take at least three pictures in the same spot. That way, if something strange appears, such as a shadow or even a figure, you can compare it to the other photos to see if there is a logical explanation.

It is also considerate to warn anyone else with you that you're about to take a photo with a flash by saying, "Flash!" That way, people know to either close their eyes or look away.

Get the Best View

While investigating a specific room, it's always wise to sit in the corner and look out into the room—that way, there's no chance of something happening behind you, and then you miss it. You can see the entire room with your back against a wall (preferably a corner). Scan the space slowly, keeping your eyes relaxed as you might see something from the corner of your eye rather than directly in front of you.

Expect to be a Little Bored

Whenever I host public events, I ask the group if they've seen any popular paranormal reality shows on TV. They often raise their hands or call out excitedly, "Yes!" My response is always the same:

"Good! Actual paranormal investigations are nothing like that!"

Where a paranormal reality show lasts about 45 minutes (with only half of it being the actual investigation), a real ghost hunt can last hours and might not be packed with excitement and activity. The truth is, ghost hunting can be pretty dull sometimes (actually, most of the time). In many instances, you're sitting in dark rooms, waiting for something to happen.

There will be moments (and possibly even entire investigations) where nothing happens. It's okay to be disappointed, but don't be discouraged! Keep exploring and trying because there may be a time when you come into contact with something supernatural, and when you do, it will all be worth it.

Don't Let Skeptics Ruin Your Experience... But It's Also Okay to be Skeptical

On almost every investigation, you'll probably have at least one person who doesn't believe in anything supernatural and doesn't even want to be there. Usually, you can spot them from a mile away. They might be rolling their eyes, scoffing, or have their arms crossed. You might hear rude remarks from them as well.

Don't let them get to you.

The paranormal is not for everyone, and that's okay.

If you can, try to avoid them. When you have time to explore on your own, go in the opposite direction they went. If a larger party is split into groups, try to get into a different one from them. And worst-case scenario, if you can't beat them, join them.

Being skeptical is actually a good thing! In fact, I encourage it. It's true you want to keep an open mind while exploring the paranormal… but not so open that your critical thinking escapes.

Not everything is a ghost—not everything that goes bump in the night, and certainly not everything captured on a camera or an audio recorder. You must question everything—try to find all the logical explanations for an experience. And when you can't, that is when things get interesting. 99% of all paranormal phenomena can be explained, making that 1% so special.

Yes, skeptics on ghost hunts can be obnoxious and even put a damper on your evening, but remember that it's always wise to keep a healthy dose of skepticism when hunting ghosts.

The Perfect EVP Session

Anytime you attend a paranormal event—whether a public hunt or a private one—you'll conduct at least one EVP session. This is a great way to get everyone present involved by asking multiple questions, but some sessions are more successful than others. Here are some tips for the perfect EVP session:

- **At the beginning of the recording, state the date, the location, and what room you're in.** This will help when you're reviewing evidence.
- **Place the recorder on a flat surface, such as a chair or table.** If you hold the recorder in your hand, any movement will create static, leading to one of two things—you think you caught something paranormal when you did not, or you won't be able to hear anything.

- **Speak in the present tense, not the past tense.** This goes along with the idea of treating the spirits like a person.
- **Don't ask the spirit how they died**—some researchers believe that not all ghosts know that they are dead and could upset them.
- **Speak in a normal voice**. If you whisper, sometimes your voice could be mistaken for an EVP. This goes for the entire investigation, not just EVP sessions. Never whisper!
- **After you ask a question, wait at least ten seconds before asking the following question (the longer, the better... some people like to wait up to a minute).** It might feel like it's taking forever, but you want to give the spirits time to respond.
- **Keep the questions simple so they don't require a long answer.** But also make sure to ask interesting questions aside from just, "What's your name?" and "How old are you?" Ghosts can

get bored by conversations, too, so keep their attention!

- **Speak one at a time.** In a larger group setting, it's best to go around the room.
- **Get creative!** Ask a spirit to count with you while you skip a few numbers to see if they fill in the blanks or ask them to finish knocking "Shave and a haircut… Two bits!"
- **Tag mundane noises.** I mentioned this in Chapter Three, but it's so important, so I'll remind you: tag noises in your EVP sessions. This could be the heat or air conditioning turning on or off, someone shifting where they're sitting or standing, a car driving by, someone sniffling and clearing their throat, someone passing gas, or even your stomach growling. If you hear it with your own ears and there's a logical/natural explanation, you'll thank yourself later for speaking up and tagging it in the recording. Nothing is worse than thinking you caught an EVP, and it's really just your teammate regretting the beef and cheese burrito they had for dinner.

A visual of what a classic EVP session looks like: the digital recorder is lying on the table with no one touching it (circled), and all three of the investigators are sitting still as they go around the table, asking questions. They tag the wind rattling the windows and the smoke detector chirping on the third floor.
Mallory Cywinski, Courtney Eastman, and Amanda Woomer at Wildwood Sanitarium, March 2022.
Photo courtesy of Hilary Opiel

Trigger Objects

You may have heard this term while watching paranormal TV, and while not everything you see on TV is true, trigger objects are a great idea to incorporate into your ghost hunt! There are a variety of trigger objects, including items, music, and clothing.

Items

Physical trigger objects can come in many forms. You might bring a ball or a doll to interact with the spirit of a child. Certain foods specific to a time, region, or culture could help stir up activity. Some people have found that bringing in old photos or antique jewelry (especially if it belonged to the spirit of the person they're trying to communicate with) has helped with their investigations. Medical supplies if you're at a hospital. A ring of jingly keys if you're in a prison. A bullet from the Civil War if you're visiting a battlefield. A religious relic such as a crucifix or an old family Bible if you're in a church.

There are no limits to trigger objects, but the more specific you can be to the location, the better—including the era of the haunting (1890s vs. 1990s).

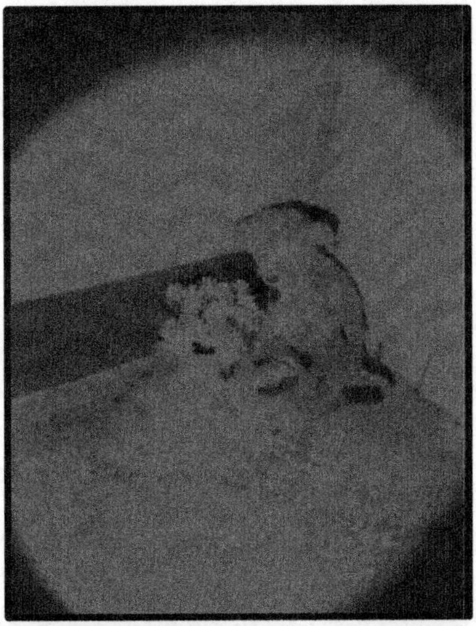

The opposite page shows four examples of trigger objects used in locations: a bear and flowers at Madison Seminary, a bear (known as the BooBuddy Jr. from GhostStop) and an old photo from the Ghostlight Theatre, offerings left to Carl at Bobby Mackey's (polaroid courtesy of Courtney Eastman), and a music box in the doll room at the Hinsdale House.

Music

Music has a way of transporting us back to a different time. Maybe you hear your favorite song from when you were ten years old, and suddenly, you're brought back to the fourth grade.

There's a theory that music can also stir up memories and energy for spirits. If you're investigating a location with ties to World War II, consider playing Glen Miller or Bing Crosby (preferably on a record if you can find one!). If you're at a location connected to the Civil War, consider playing or even singing *The Battle Hymn of the Republic* or *When Johnny Comes Marching Home*. These songs will be familiar to the location's ghosts which will catch their attention and might help them trust you more (leading to a better investigation).

Incorporating music into your investigation goes along with the idea that louder noises can stir up energy. This could be by playing an instrument, singing, or simply speaking loudly. [Please note, though, that speaking loudly does not mean shouting, as this could be interpreted as being aggressive, and spirits might not want to interact with you.]

> **FUN FACT:** During Victorian séances and even Spiritualist church services today, participants begin by singing joyfully to raise the energy level of the room.

While investigating a former German church, my group sat up in the old choir balcony and started softly singing *Stille Nacht* (*Silent Night* in German). The rest of the night was filled with activity (including an incredible EVP and photo).

Before you start singing or playing big band music, ask permission if it's okay (especially if you're on a public investigation). Not everyone will be open to the idea, so this might be an experiment you must save until you're on a private investigation.

Clothing

One of the best ways that you can really add to your ghost hunting experience is by dressing in period-style clothing. This idea suggests that dressing up in the proper clothes for the time of a particular haunting makes you appear safer to ghosts and can lead to a more personal and meaningful interaction. By donning the appropriate attire, hairstyle, and even mannerisms, you can blend into the supernatural surroundings—instead of "hunting" ghosts, you can interact with them on a more human level.

If you're visiting Fort Mifflin, young men might wear the iconic "red coat" of the 18th Century British Army. While exploring Antietam or Gettysburg, ladies could try putting on a bonnet and Victorian dress (hoop skirt is optional!). If a spirit is from World War II, try to put your hair in victory rolls, and if you're working with a ghost from the 1990s, then low-rise jeans, a Spice Girls shirt, a henna choker, and butterfly clips are a must!

This idea (along with other trigger objects) goes back to treating ghosts like people and acknowledging the things that mattered to them in life.

An actress portraying the Lady in Red at the Ghostlight Theatre in New York as part of a public ghost tour.

Left: Deanna Erskine dressed in a period nightgown at Wilson Castle.
Right: Alex Matsuo dressed in a Civil War Era dress in Gettysburg.

It's Okay to Leave

If at any point you get scared, it is perfectly fine to remove yourself from the situation. If you're on a public ghost hunt, find the person in charge and explain to them that you are scared and need to leave. Many times, there is a home base where you can go to relax and calm down.

It is vital to try to stay calm. You don't want to run away—you could hurt yourself, and you don't want to wander off alone. Look to the adults in charge who are there to ensure you have a safe and fun experience.

While taking a break, stop and ask yourself what made you nervous or scared. Once you realize what triggered this reaction, you can start to come up with ways to help next time (if it was the dark, maybe carry around a flashlight).

These experiences—while not enjoyable at the moment—can be beneficial down the road. You might be able to help another young person with a similar response, or if you feel nervous again, you can push yourself and overcome that fear. And don't feel embarrassed: even adults who have been doing this for years get scared sometimes!

You Don't have to Investigate in the Dark

No one says you must investigate in the pitch black—some people might be afraid of the dark, while others might not want to have to worry about falling down stairs or tripping over uneven floors. Plus, if you're hoping to see something paranormal, how will you see it if it's dark? Some people rely heavily on night-vision cameras (which start at only $50). However, there is a cheaper and safer option that might make things more enjoyable for you.

Consider dimly lighting your space. This could be in the form of lanterns, light-up cubes (night lights for little kids), or using overhead lights on a dimmer switch. You want to make sure it's still a bit dark so you can see any equipment that lights up when giving a reading. But if you can see a bit better, you might notice an object moving on its own or see a shadow, light anomaly, or even a full-body apparition you might have missed in the dark.

Cleansing

Just as some people like to spiritually protect themselves before visiting a haunted location, as mentioned in Chapter Six, many people want to cleanse after an investigation as well. This is due to the idea that a ghost could possibly attach itself to you and follow you home. Personally, I like visiting haunted locations, but I don't want to live in one. So if you'd rather not bring home an invisible roommate that mom and dad might not want around, here are some tips to properly cleanse after a ghost hunt:

> **FUN FACT:** Some ghost lore claims that spirits cannot cross water, so if you go over a bridge on your way home, you might be good!

- **Set boundaries.** It might sound simple, but it works. Just like you might set boundaries with a living person, you can also set them with spirits, and usually, they comply. Before I leave any location, I thank the spirits and inform them that they cannot follow me home, they are not welcome at my house, and they need to stay where they are. So far, this has worked for me.

- **Smoke Cleanse.** I have a palo santo stick in my car that I immediately light after a hunt and purify the air around me. You can also use incense, which is relatively affordable at your local metaphysical shop. Dragon's blood is a popular incense that is associated with protection. Cedar is used for purification, rosemary for home protection, clove to remove negativity, sandalwood for protection, and juniper for spiritual protection.
- **Bells.** It's believed that sound can purify and change the energy of a specific area. You might notice that many metaphysical shops have windchimes or small bells on their doors that ring as you enter. This isn't just to let the employee know that a customer has arrived but to cleanse the energy they brought in with them. I have a small bell that I hang on the door of my house, and every time I return from a ghost hunt and hear it ring, I know that if anything was latched onto me, at that point, it has been cleansed.

- **A shower.** After a ghost hunt, you'll probably want to shower to get the dirt and dust off you. But a shower is also an excellent way to help cleanse your spirit and energy. As the water runs over your body, visualize the energy of the haunted location falling away from you like mud.
- **Shake it off.** A popular crystal that is cheap in its natural unpolished form, selenite wands are perfect for helping rid yourself of unwanted energy. Hold the crystal above our skin and begin scrubbing the energy away. Another option is a tiny broom (like the cinnamon brooms they sell during the holidays). Use it to sweep the energy off your body—this is something I do each morning to remove the energy from the previous day and start fresh. Lastly, you can shake the energy off of you before you step inside your house.
- **Prayer.** Some people might like to say a prayer before they leave a location. This could be to God, angels, your spirit guides, loved ones who

have passed away, your ancestors, or another deity of your choice.

- **Holy water.** It might seem a bit dramatic to some, but there are people who carry holy water with them on investigations and use it to cleanse themselves before leaving a location. Even some haunted places offer holy water as you leave (though these tend to be the places that push the "demon" narrative).

Simple (cheap) tools you can use: selenite wand, palo santo, dragon's blood incense stick, small broom.

It's important to remember to purify the tools you used after a cleansing. The most common way to do this is by placing them in the light of a full moon. Other ways include using smoke, bells, and clear quartz.

Leave No Trace

This should be a no-brainer and (like so many things) not just regarding the paranormal.

The majority of haunted locations are historic landmarks (some of them are even on the National Register of Historic Places), and because of that, they need to be taken care of. And even if they aren't a well-known historic location, you should still treat it (and the people who own it) with respect.

If you brought food in, take any leftovers home with you. Some of the lesser kept locations have animals such as mice, squirrels, bats, raccoons, and opossums living in attics and cellars, and food left lying around could lure them out and cause a health and safety issue (not to mention the owners will have to clean up the animals' mess and yours).

If you have any trash—food wrappers, battery packages, tissues, etc.—throw them away. Most locations have a garbage can in their base camp area, so use it.

If you move any furniture around during your investigation, put it back how you found it.

Many owners of haunted locations will remember investigators. You want to make a good impression if you want to come back for a second visit.

Consider Returning

You might not always be able to return to a location—perhaps you traveled a long distance for a dream destination, and that's your one shot. However, if you can ever go back to a haunted location, I highly recommend you do.

The more time you spend in a location, your results might be better. The spirits recognize you and might interact a bit more, or perhaps your nerves from a first-time visit are gone, and you can get a better feel for the location.

My first time at Wildwood Sanitarium was eerily quiet—not a creak in the 100-year-old floors, no EVPs, and no uneasy feelings. The second time I visited, we heard knocking, phantom footsteps on the floor above us (when no one else was up there), balls moved on their own, and we even saw shadows.

Many times, the success of a ghost hunt has a lot to do with your group, so if something feels "off" about the people you're with, you might want to return with a different group.

Consider a Daytime Investigation

When most people imagine a ghost hunt, they instantly think of a spooky location in the middle of the night. Why?

Most investigations are held overnight simply because the majority of ghost hunters (even the better-known ones) work during the day. Ghost hunting is not a full-time job, so most investigators work during the day and have time to investigate at night. Some of the interactive gadgets, such as K2 meters, REM-Pods, and even cat balls, incorporate lights in their designs, so it's ideal to use them in the dark. Nighttime also provides less noise pollution, such as cars driving by and people talking or shouting outside.

While many paranormal investigations do occur at night, there's no reason why you can't investigate during the day. In fact, many ghostly encounters people report at haunted locations happen during the day while they're doing something mundane and not actively looking for ghosts.

One theory suggests that you must get on their schedule if you want to see a ghost. Most living things are active during the day and sleep at night, so if you're hoping to experience a haunting—either intelligent or residual—then you might want to try it while the ghost (who in theory was once a living person) is "awake."

While investigating Madison Seminary, our daytime investigation was much more active than our nighttime one.

Daytime investigations are preferred if you're visiting a haunted road since drivers are more likely to see you, and it is significantly safer. Also, if you're planning on investigating a cemetery, most are only open from dawn until dusk, so to avoid trespassing, you'll have to go during the day.

These are just a few tips and tricks for a successful ghost hunt—some things will work for you, and some might not. As you continue to visit haunted locations and go on both public and private hunts, you'll eventually figure out your own personal approach, which is essential. No one can tell you what to think or believe within the paranormal… this is a personal journey where you must seek the answers for yourself.

You should always stop and sit in an old bathtub inside a haunted bathhouse.

The final tip for you is to have fun and not take yourself (or ghost hunting) too seriously. If you stop and think about what we do—sit in freezing cold/sweltering hot buildings in the dark, while asking questions to thin air, hoping an invisible being answers us—it can seem pretty funny. So always make sure you're enjoying yourself, because if you're not, then what's the point?

Chapter Eight
Reviewing Evidence

Remember how I said that ghost hunting could be boring? Well, welcome to the most boring part of paranormal investigating—evidence review! Luckily, this is not something you have to do right away, so you can give your mind and body time to recover from your overnight (the older you get, the longer it takes to bounce back… trust me). Some investigators have months and even years of evidence they still haven't reviewed (myself included), so don't feel bad if it takes you a while to sit down and look at your photos, listen to audio, and watch videos.

Photos

Taking photos is one of the easiest ways to collect potential evidence on a ghost hunt. There are several ways you can do this. The first is using the camera on your phone (as mentioned in Chapter Four). The second option is a digital camera. The third is a film camera such as a Polaroid or disposable camera.

There are pros and cons to digital versus film, and many investigators use a combination of both (I like to use my phone as well as a Polaroid camera). Some people believe that the chemicals in Polaroid film can pick up specific energies better than digital cameras. However, photos printed from film are harder to examine since you can't zoom in without uploading them to a computer.

When scanning a photo for anything out of the ordinary, I recommend one of two ways:

1. Start in the upper left corner and make your way across to the right, then slide down a bit, go from right to left, slide down, left to right, etc., until you reach the bottom.
2. Start at the top and scan the photo clockwise along the outside. Once you're back at the top,

slide down a bit and repeat until you're in the middle.

This can be done on a computer or with a magnifying glass on physical prints. If you think you may have caught something, try to get the photo on a larger screen and look for a second opinion from someone you trust.

Remember that not everything you catch on film that seems paranormal is actually paranormal. Most of the time, things like mists, orbs, and even faces in windows/mirrors are not a sign of paranormal activity. As mentioned in Chapter Three, 99% of the time, orbs are nothing more than moisture, precipitation, dust, or bugs. Mists can also have very natural explanations, such as fog, moisture, and even seeing your breath when it's cold outside. Faces appearing in windows, mirrors, and other surfaces are not proof of ghosts but proof of matrixing (the phenomenon of our brains trying to see faces and make patterns out of chaos). This is also called pareidolia.

FUN FACT: The most famous case of pareidolia is the man in the moon.

AUDIO

Depending on how many EVP sessions you conducted (or if you placed a recorder down and left it alone for some time), you might have hours of work ahead of you.

When reviewing audio, I like to get the files onto my computer. Audacity is a free audio editing software program and an excellent resource for you—it allows you to watch the sound waves on the screen (sometimes helping you pinpoint a potential EVP) and has helpful tools such as "amplify" (making the audio louder) and "noise reduction" (which helps get rid of the annoying white noise usually heard in the background of recordings).

Some tips for reviewing audio recordings:

- **Find a quiet place.** You'll want to sit and listen to your audio without any distractions or interruptions. Make sure you tell your parents or siblings what you're doing so they know not to disturb you.
- **Use headphones.** EVPs tend to be very quiet, sometimes hidden among regular conversations, so you'll want to be able to listen as closely as

possible. Make sure you don't use noise-canceling headphones, though, because they can sometimes filter out possible EVPs.

- **Listen for anything that might seem out of place.** EVPs can come in the form of voices, knocking, music, footsteps, and bangs.
- **Have a notebook next to you.** You'll want to write down the timestamp of potential EVPs so you can go back and review them.
- **Take a break.** Listening to audio recordings can be mind-numbing and give you a headache after a while. You're also on high alert, and your ears might be on edge where everything sounds like an EVP. Take a break and continue when your head is clear, and your ears have relaxed.

Generally, it's not ideal to edit/alter an audio recording too much. The more you tamper with the file, the more chances people will have to question its authenticity, so be sure to leave the file as close to the original as possible.

Some investigators categorize their EVPs as Class A, B, or C. Not everyone does this, as any EVP is impressive, but if you'd like to, here are the guidelines that most investigators follow:

Class A: The EVP is loud and clear. Most (if not all) people come to the same conclusion about what is said. You don't have to point out where the EVP is in the recording.

Class B: The EVP is a bit quiet or mumbled, but you can still understand it with some amplifying and noise reduction. It may be more difficult for someone not experienced with listening to EVPs to make out on their own.

Class C: The EVP is quiet and difficult to make out. You might not be able to understand what is said at all… all you know is that there is something there.

VIDEO

It can be a bit overwhelming when looking at video recording devices. You have your basic camcorder as well as thermal-imaging cameras, SLS, full-spectrum, and infrared (night vision). If you want to add a camera to your ghost hunting equipment, you'll likely want to start with one equipped with night vision since they're significantly cheaper than more advanced cameras.

Some people like to walk around with a camcorder in their hands (which can sometimes lead to blurry footage), so place your camera on a tripod pointed at a specific paranormal hot spot and leave it alone.

Keep in mind that the more you record, the more you have to review. And the more cameras you have with you, the review period will be even longer. Don't let that dissuade you! Just be prepared to spend hours looking at dark, empty rooms and hallways.

Here are some tips for reviewing video evidence:

- **Try to get your video onto the biggest screen possible.** That means don't just watch it on your camcorder. You should transfer the files to your computer and, if possible, project the video onto your TV. People can miss potential evidence if the screen is too small.
- **Take notes.** Have a notebook and pen next to you to make a note of anything strange or unusual.
- **Beware of "orbs."** Even famous ghost hunting shows can't resist the allure of the orb. Video evidence often comes in the form of small balls or rods of light. Remember that you're most

likely investigating in an old, dusty building or outside with bugs and moisture in the air.

- **Take breaks when needed.** Just like reviewing audio evidence, reviewing video footage can get really old really fast. Take breaks as often as you need. Remember, it's not a race, so you don't have to force yourself to get through it as fast as possible. If you do, you might miss something in the video.
- **Ask for a second opinion.** This is a good rule in many aspects of the paranormal. As you continue to learn and grow in the field, you'll get to know people that you look up to and respect. Always go to them for a second opinion to see if you truly caught something paranormal.
- **Avoid editing clips.** Once you've reviewed everything on a bigger screen, you might want to play with it on your computer. Be careful. Like photos and audio, the less you do to potential evidence, the better. You could try to raise the volume or lighten the video, but that's all you

should do. Anything more and your evidence could become suspicious.

Chapter Nine
The Paranormal Community

Joining the Community

One of the best things about investigating the paranormal is the people (aka the fellow weirdos) you'll get to know along the way. Now that's not to say that some people out there might not want to work with you (and some might not even like you). But most researchers and investigators are interested in having new people join the community to see what new ideas, theories, experiments, and experiences they can bring to the field.

If your parents are okay with it, I recommend making several social media accounts for your paranormal work to connect with people in the field—fellow teens, more seasoned investigators, and even para-celebrities all have accounts you can follow, learn from, and sometimes even ask questions.

Get Creative in the Community

There are so many ways to get involved with the paranormal community. After you've gotten your toes wet by attending several investigations, you might want to share your experiences (or, if you're lucky, your evidence) with others. With your parent's permission, you could:

- Start a blog
- Start a podcast
- Make videos for Youtube or TikTok
- Submit articles for various magazines and journals such as *The Feminine Macabre*, *Haunted Magazine,* and *Paranormality.*
- Write a book

Other Ways to Explore the Paranormal

If you're unable to make it to ghost hunts regularly (let's be honest, they take up lots of time and cost a bit of money), there are other ways to still be part of the paranormal community and explore everything it has to offer.

Library Talks

Most libraries offer tons of free events throughout the year for the community, and around Halloween time, those events tend to get spooky. These talks are usually hosted by a paranormal investigator or haunted historian and are a great way to learn a bit of ghost hunting 101 or even some local legends and lore! Keep an eye on your library's website or social media for these events. You could also always request an event like this.

Ghost Walks

A bit more laid back than a ghost hunt, ghost walks (or ghost tours) are another fun way to get to know the stories and legends of a specific place. Depending on the location, there are tons of tours to choose from (cities like New Orleans, Salem, Key West, and Gettysburg almost always have tours running). This is also a fun way to introduce others to the paranormal—they might not have the nerve to go on an investigation, but they might be able to handle a tour!

Paracons

Paracons and conferences are fantastic ways to see people within the community in real life. There are different types of paracons:

One style focuses on celebrity meet and greets, such as the New Jersey Paraunity Expo in Woodbridge, New Jersey.

Others focus on speakers and research, such as Troy Taylor's Haunted America Conference in Alton, Illinois.

Many haunted locations have their own paracons to help raise money, so paracons are accessible to most in the paranormal community.

Check Out Podcasts

There are hundreds of podcasts dedicated solely to ghosts and hauntings—even more about cryptids, aliens, and other Fortean topics. A great way to interact with creators in the paranormal community while learning lots of new stuff is by checking out as many podcasts as possible.

Paraunity

It's a term you might see from time to time, and it's a nice idea—all of the weirdos working together to find answers in the mysterious world of the supernatural. But the truth is that not everyone in the paranormal community gets along… and that's okay. There are different approaches to investigating and different theories of what the paranormal actually is. Throw in people competing for screen time on TV shows and followers on social media, and you've got a field that is anything but unified. And again, that's okay.

I advise you to find the people you connect with and stick with them. We can learn and grow with one another without being focused on "paraunity."

The most important thing to remember while on your paranormal journey is to be on it for yourself, not others. Many times, paranormal investigators, researchers, and content creators start comparing themselves (and their "success" in the form of likes, comments, and follows) to others in the community. It's difficult not to do this, especially in the age of social media, but try your best (even I struggle with this sometimes).

Search the paranormal for answers for yourself, not others… because questions about life and death (and what potentially comes next) are so personal. Only you can find the right answer for yourself, just as others can only find the right answer for themselves.

Try to find evidence of ghosts and spirits for yourself… because not everyone will be impressed with what you've caught.

The moment you stop exploring the paranormal for yourself and try to create, perform, or wonder for others, it stops being fun, and you can become discouraged.

My advice to you is this:

Your paranormal journey is yours and yours alone. Always remain curious. Never stop asking questions. Read as many books as you can. Keep an open mind. Stay true to yourself. Be respectful. Have fun.

Chapter Ten
Recommended Reading

You've made it through this book… now what? There are hundreds (possibly even thousands) of books on the paranormal. Not just ghosts but cryptids, aliens, unexplained phenomena, witchcraft, tarot, astrology, and the occult. Where should you go next?

Here are some of my favorite books that belong in every ghost hunter's spooky library:

Bagans, Zak. (2020). *Ghost-Hunting for Dummies*. John Wiley & Sons, Inc.

Belanger, Michelle (2009). *The Ghost Hunter's Survival Guide: Protection Techniques for Encounters with the Paranormal*. Llewellyn Publications.

Block, Courtney M. (2020). *Researching the Paranormal: How to Find Reliable Information about Parapsychology, Ghosts, Astrology, Cryptozoology, Near-Death Experiences, and More.* Rowman & Littlefield.

Cross, J. Allen (2022). *Witch's Guide to the Paranormal: How to Investigate, Communicate, and Clear Spirits*. Llewellyn Publications.

Crowe, Catherine. (2011). *The Night-Side of Nature: Or, Ghosts and Ghost Seers*. Forgotten Books.

Goodchild, Claire. (2022). *The Book of Séances.* Hachette UK Distribution Ltd.

Guiley, Rosemary. (2009). *The Encyclopedia of Ghosts and Spirits.* Facts on File.

Martin Ellis, Melissa. (2014). *The Everything Ghost Hunting Book: Tips, Tools, and Techniques for Exploring the Supernatural World.* Adams Media.

Matsuo, Alex. (2019). *The Brave Mortal's Guide to Ghost Hunting.* Independently Published.

Newman, Rich. (2011). *Ghost Hunting for Beginners: Everything You Need to Know to Get Started.* Llewellyn Publications.

Paradis, Sean. (2019). *Low-Tech Ghost Hunting 101.* Independently Published.

Stevenson, Paul. (Editor). *Haunted Magazine.*

Taylor, Troy. (Editor). *The Morbid Curious.*

Woomer, Amanda. (2021). *The Feminine Macabre: A Woman's Journal of All Things Strange and Unusual.* Volumes 1-4. Spook-Eats Publishing.

Acknowledgments

Several teams and individuals offered to help with this book (and by doing so, offered to help you at the beginning of your paranormal journey). I want to thank them for helping me with this project and introduce you to them. That way, you won't be alone as you take your first steps on your paranormal journey.

Mike Caprio (@mik3caprio)

Richard Estep (@estepr)

Missy Lathrop (Paranormal Five)

Alex Matsuo (@TheSpookyStuff)

Greg Morrill (@theallthewierd)

Michele Smith

@AHedgewitch

BJ of The Unrefined Podcast (@BJtheWebGuy)

Leanne of UK Paranormal Society (@Ghostess_Leanne)

References:

A&E Television Networks. (2009). *History of Ghost Stories*. History.com. www.history.com/.amp/topics/halloween/historical-ghost-stories

Block, C.M. (2020). *Researching the Paranormal: How to Find Reliable Information about Parapsychology, Ghosts, Astrology, Cryptozoology, Near-Death Experiences, and More.* Rowman & Littlefield.

Estep, R. (2020). *A Nightmare in Villisca: Investigating the Haunted Axe Murder House*.

Everett, F. (2021, May 15). *Have you ever experienced a time slip?* Daily Mail Online. Retrieved November 6, 2022, from https://www.dailymail.co.uk/home/you/article-9565865/Have-experienced-time-slip.html

Gershon, L. (2021, October 22). *3,500-Year-Old Babylonian Tablet May Contain Earliest Known Depiction of a Ghost.* Smithsonian.com. www.smithsonianmag.com/smart-news/3500-year-old-babylonian-tablet-may-hold-earliest-known-ghost-image-180978923

Ghost stories. George Washington's Mount Vernon. (n.d.). Retrieved November 6, 2022, from https://www.mountvernon.org/preservation/mount-vernon-ladies-association/mount-vernon-through-time/ghost-stories/

Goodchild, C. (2022). *The Book of Séances.* Hachette UK Distribution Ltd.

Greene County Poor Farm Ghost hunt. Ghost Hunts USA | Ghost Hunts | Ghost Hunting Events | Haunted | Paranormal. (2022, July 20). Retrieved November 6, 2022, from https://ghosthuntsusa.com/haunted-locations/greene-county-poor-farm-ghost-hunt/

Guiley, R.E. (2009). *The Encyclopedia of Demons and Demonology.* Checkbooks.

Guiley, R.E. (2009). *The Encyclopedia of Ghosts and Spirits.* Facts on File.

Haunting phenomena: The smell of ghosts. Journal News. (2022, May 27). Retrieved November 6, 2022, from https://journalnews.com.ph/haunting-phenomena-the-smell-of-ghosts/

Hill, S. (2018, January 29). *Spooky Rocks*. Skeptical Inquirer. Retrieved November 6, 2022, from https://skepticalinquirer.org/newsletter/spooky-rocks/

Hill View's History. Haunted Hill View Manor. (2021, December 14). Retrieved November 6, 2022, from https://hauntedhillviewmanor.com/about-hill-view-manor/

Mark, J. J. (2022, November 4). *Ghosts in the Middle Ages*. World History Encyclopedia. Retrieved November 6, 2022, from https://www.worldhistory.org/article/1404/ghosts-in-the-middle-ages/

Matsuo, A. (2019). *The Brave Mortal's Guide to Ghost Hunting.* Independently Published.

Merriam-Webster. (n.d.). *Demon definition & meaning*. Merriam-Webster. Retrieved November 6, 2022, from https://www.merriam-webster.com/dictionary/demon

Newman, R. (2011). *Ghost Hunting for Beginners: Everything You Need to Know to Get Started.* Llewellyn Publications.

Night at Ashmore Estates. AMERICAN HAUNTINGS GHOST HUNTS. (n.d.). Retrieved November 6, 2022, from https://www.bumpinthenight.net/ashmore

Pliny the Younger (1909–14). "LXXXIII. To Sura." In Charles W. Eliot (ed.). *Letters, by Pliny the Younger; translated by William Melmoth; revised by F. C. T. Bosanquet*. The Harvard Classics. Vol. 9. New York: P.F. Collier & Son.

Tenney, J.E.L. (2022). *Why Cassette Recorders are Better for EVPs.*

Walker, T. (2020, August 4). *Five chilling instances of Time Slips*. Medium. Retrieved November 6, 2022, from https://medium.com/inside-the-simulation/five-chilling-instances-of-time-slips-d3a7248c9e09

Woomer, A., Matsuo, A., Goodchild, C., and Williams, C. (2021). *The Feminine Macabre: A Woman's Journal of All Things Strange and Unusual.* Spook-Eats Publishing.

Woomer, A., Bennett, A, Casseday, A.. (2021). *The Feminine Macabre Volume II.* Spook-Eats Publishing.

About the Author

Writer, anthropologist, and paranormal researcher, Amanda R. Woomer was born and raised in Buffalo, NY. The owner of Spook-Eats, she is a featured writer for *Haunted Magazine*, *The Morbid Curious*, and the curator of the all-female paranormal journal, *The Feminine Macabre*. She is the author of eleven other books for kids and adults, including *The Spirit Guide* series, *A Very Frightful Victorian Christmas*, and *The Cryptid ABC Book*. Follow her spooky adventures at spookeats.com and on Facebook, Instagram, and Twitter. To learn more about *The Feminine Macabre*, you can find them on Facebook and Instagram @the.feminine.macabre.

Printed in Great Britain
by Amazon

45878886R00076